A REBEL'S JOURNEY:

My path to liberty

Darryl W. Perry

A REBEL'S JOURNEY:

My path to liberty

Darryl W. Perry

FPP.cc

FREE PRESS PUBLICATIONS

Published by Free Press Publications
http://FPP.cc

ISBN: 1-9383572-1-3
ISBN 13: 978-1-938357-21-3

Printed with the spirit of  &

http://agorist.org   http://voluntaryist.com

FREE PRESS PUBLICATIONS

Free Press Publications is an independent alternative media / publishing company, founded in June 2009, with the mission of "ensuring a FREE PRESS for the FREEDOM MOVEMENT" and to also give new authors an avenue for publishing freedom oriented material.

Table of Contents

Dedication

To everyone who, at some point in my life, helped me along my path to the ideas of liberty, even if it was unknowingly. To everyone who has provided emotional support to me along my path, and especially to those who have provided support and encouragement for me to finish this book, which took longer than expected, but wouldn't have been the same if it had been finished three years ago.

A special thank you to:
Suzanna Nope, Bonnie Pizza, Michael Williammee, Cody Towner, Rhonda Williammee, Jordan Weaver, Nate Danielson, and Donna Slopey for donating to the fund-raiser to help get this book into more hands!

INTRODUCTION

It all began on a Tuesday morning in February 1978, Chinese New Year – the Year of the Horse – it was also the day I was born. Born to a twenty-one year old father who was working as a manager at Shoney's and a nineteen year old mother who had dropped out of high school after she became pregnant with my brother.

It was nearly three decades later that I would learn my journey did not begin on that Tuesday morning, it did not begin months earlier when I was conceived, my journey began several hundred years ago. My journey began when William Swinhoe (Swindle) decided to board a ship with his family, leave his home in England and settle in Jamestowne. When William's great grandchildren fought in the French & Indian Wars and their children fought in the American Revolution, my journey was continuing. When my distant cousin James Madison was writing the Constitution of these United States of America, my journey was continuing. My journey continued as my ancestors fought to defend their new country from the British during the War of 1812 and continued on as my great-great-great grandfather John Henry Myers joined the 10th Alabama Cavalry and fought to protect his land from invasion. My journey is not my own, rather my journey belongs to everyone past, present & future that has had the courage to stand up for what they feel is right in the face of oppression and perceived wrong doing. My journey is a rebel's journey.

What happened after being born on that Tuesday morning, is partly clouded in mystery. According to one of my parents, I spent the next several months in the hospital due to being born prematurely. However, according to one of my grandmothers that was not the case, I was simply dealing with a bout of jaundice. Whether or not I spent much (if any) time in a hospital after birth is irrelevant. What mattered is that I had a family that loved me and wanted the best for me, or so it seemed.

Before I turned two my parents had divorced and I, along with my brother, spent the next few years bouncing between parents & grandparents from both sides of the family before landing in my father's custody. I have no memory of this or much of anything before I was four or five years old. Though growing up, my Mamaw (that's a southern term for grandmother) would often tell about the time I was standing on a chair at the kitchen table as she was cooking – something she did often and very well (she has the ability to recite any recipe from memory at the drop of a hat) – she turned to me and said, "now you sit down before you fall out of that chair and crack your head wide open!" As I sat down, I fell out of the chair and cracked my head open on an exposed door hinge. She picked me up, called the doctor to have him meet us at his office – something that was not uncommon in the early 1980's – as he was stitching my head I'm told I looked up and saw some of my blood on my grandmother's chin and said "Mamaw, you've got blood on your chin." The doctor and Mamaw had a bit of a laugh as the doctor replied, "poor child is bleeding half to death and he's worried about his Mamaw."

A Rebel's Journey

I'm also told that around the same age I told her, "Mamaw, one day I'm going to buy you a red Cadillac." Though how or why I made this promise at a young age is still a mystery to me; I still intend on being able to buy her that red Cadillac, one day.

Among my first memories; I recall my father making slushies in a blender using ice cubes and kool-aid. My brother and I would then take them to the neighbors in the apartment complex. When the weather would get warmer, we'd have water balloon fights or swim in the pool. As I couldn't yet swim, I had a Bugs Bunny floaty that I used to hold me up. I remember one day sliding out of the floaty and sinking to the bottom of the pool. I can still see in my memory as clear as a picture, looking down on myself from above, as my body sank deeper into the pool, I rose higher into the sky. I watched myself being pulled out of the pool and revived. Many years later, I asked my father about this, "did it really happen or did I dream that it happened?" He was surprised I knew about this incident, he knew that he'd never told me this story and neither had my brother; he asked me how I knew about it, and told me to never mention it again.

Not long afterwards (it could have been weeks or even months, I'm not quite sure), we moved from that apartment into a small two bedroom house in the East Lake neighborhood of Birmingham, Alabama. The first day in our new house the power wasn't working. My father had my brother and me ask the neighbors if their power was working – so that he could determine if there was a local outage or the power company had simply forgotten to turn on our power. I don't remember whether or not they had power, however I do remember being given some fresh baked cookies. Over the next few months, the next door neighbor had introduced my father to his sister. A lovely woman that wanted children and was unable to have any of her own. My father joked that she only married him because of me and my

3

brother. Judy was an amazing woman, though she did not give birth to me, because of her love and devotion to my brother and me, she was "Mom."

While living in East Lake, my father – who quit a job working for the Alabama Department of Transportation to work for himself – operated a concession stand at a local park selling drinks, snacks & renting out paddle boats. He was truly a small business owner. Unable to hire people to work for him; Judy, my brother & I were his employees. I learned to count before entering school by helping run that concession stand. I couldn't do much, though I was able to sit on a stool at the window and count change. That would never be allowed today, because governments have placed so many regulations against both child labor and food safety. The horrors of a 5 year old child counting change and handing someone a bag of chips. For the next several years, we continued selling snacks, drinks and renting paddle boats at East Lake Park. My father's concession business even expanded to the local YMCA, selling snacks at the youth league soccer games.

My brother loved playing soccer, I did not – though I was signed up for a team anyways. I always played defense, which meant I stood in a small little area near the goalie box and didn't do anything until the ball was kicked in my general direction. If you've ever seen a youth soccer game you know that most of the time everyone except the goalies and 1 or two players on defense are huddled in a small area chasing the soccer ball and the ball rarely leaves that mass of children. You can now, hopefully, understand my boredom with the game. I found basketball and BMX racing to be much more fun. Of course, that was before BMX was on ESPN. It was essentially racing a bicycle on a dirt course with a couple of hills, nothing fancy, though I always had fun.

A Rebel's Journey

Another fond childhood memory involved football. My great-grandmother lived only one block from Legion Field in Birmingham. For many years both major colleges in the state (Alabama & Auburn) played their home games in that stadium; though Auburn would also play games at their on campus stadium, Jordan-Hare. Legion Field was also the home stadium for the Birmingham Stallions of the USFL – a league that was supposed to rival the NFL, and in some ways did. Almost every Saturday during the fall was spent at Grandmother Hamilton's house parking cars. I'd stand on the street corner waving either my hand, a towel or a pom-pom directing cars either to the drive way, behind or beside another car. "Five dollars! Parking is only five dollars!" I'd shout at the cars driving down the street. For as far as you could see in any direction, people were parking cars in their yards. Everyone charged the same to park, though not everyone would actually watch the cars to ensure they weren't broken into. We did and no one ever had a car broken into or a tire slashed at Grandmother Hamilton's house. We had several families that were regular customers, they always arrived at the same time and parked in the same place.

As a child there are certain things you don't realize until years later. I never realized that my great-grandmother and the neighbor that lived across the alley were the only two white people that lived in that neighborhood. I didn't realize that just a few blocks away was one of the most dangerous projects in the city. As a child I knew all of the neighbors and played with their children. I didn't care that their skin was darker than mine.

After I was old enough to drive, my brother was in college and my father was no longer helping park cars, I was able to do the job myself. One day in particular, the University of Alabama had played an early game, the last cars had left and I was standing in the alley talking to the neighbor when a Police Officer on horse rode up to us and said "it's getting late and this neighborhood is pretty bad, you may want to think about leaving now." I didn't think for even a second and replied, "my grandmother lives in this house," pointing back to her house, "and she lives in this house," pointing at hers, "I come out here almost every weekend. I know this neighborhood and I've never had a problem." With that reply, he rode away. Today, a reply of that sort would likely end with me being pepper-sprayed, tazed or arrested, or any combination of the three.

This was not my first time to question authority. I've never been the type of person to accept "because I said so" as a valid answer. When I was a teenager and attended church regularly, I would often question the Sunday School teachers about why certain things are different now than they were. The Church of Christ, where my dad's parent went to church, would not play musical instruments while singing hymns. I remember asking a Sunday School teacher about this and mentioned that angels played trumpets, David played a lyre and there are other references to people playing drums and cymbals. Her response: "you don't put jelly on the communion bread." Other church leaders would often talk about the need to support traditional values, but would never go into detail about those values.

I've always been curious about the how's and why's and have always sought the truth. It was this quest for truth and a definition of traditional values that has led me to where I am today and drives me on my journey.

As a talk show host, one of the questions I like to ask my guests is: "how did you come to the ideas of liberty?"

I've come to realize that there is rarely ever one specific thing or event that people can pinpoint as *the beginning* of their path towards liberty. The same is true of me.

A Rebel's Journey

As a child I remember my father teaching to me to question what I believed. I recall an instance in which he had several paddle boats in the front yard of our suburban home, and a neighbor called the cops to report a zoning violation. I knew something wasn't right when people could call the cops for someone having a boat in their yard. Of course, this was two and a half decades ago, well before people were being arrested for having gardens instead of grass. It wasn't long after this incident that my father decided to run for City Council. During his campaign, he, my brother, and I walked neighborhoods knocking on doors handing out business cards. I don't remember any part of my father's platform or the exact results, other than the fact that he lost the election, but I do remember a valuable lesson: if you don't like the way things are, try to change them.

Several years later when I was in junior high and high school, I remember learning how the government works, or at least the watered down version they taught in school in the 1990's. I learned a watered-down version of American history from 1776-1791, and all of the excuses given for why a powerful central government was needed to replace the Articles of Confederation.

The 1992 Presidential election was during my Freshman year. I remember being really excited about Ross Perot's candidacy. He made sense, and was a businessman. At the time, as the national debt was approaching $4 trillion, I thought that was what the country needed. I recall being one of the few people in my history class (where these ideas were actually discussed) to support Perot. Few in the class supported Clinton, with most of the class supporting Bush. There were 8 candidates on the ballot in Alabama (Bush, Clinton, Perot, Andre Marrou, Lenore Fulani, James Warren, Lyndon LaRouche & John Hagelin), we weren't even informed that any of these other candidates were running.

Darryl W. Perry

During my Junior and Senior years of high school, I was on the debate team and learned to examine issues from both sides. It was during this time that I learned there were multiple sides to the issues. I began to see things with an open mind and began researching the history of laws as they existed at the time. Even though I was not ideologically a libertarian when I graduated high school, I was on my way.

It was during my college years that I first learned the real history of the War on Drugs. There was no FDA until the early 1900's. cannabis, cocaine, and many other drugs could be ordered from the Sears catalog, but drug abuse was not any more prevalent than it is today. The War on Drugs began because of yellow journalism and racism.

I remember asking myself, "if I was lied to about the Drug War, what else have I been told that was a lie?"

Around the same time, while attending church in the late 90's, I remember one of the deacons saying that "we need to have a government that supports traditional values." Though he was unable to explain in detail what he meant.

I decided to find out what "traditional values" actually were. It was a long process, but it was a process well worth the effort, that led me down the path from conservative to conservative libertarian to constitutionalist to constitutional libertarian to voluntaryist; and can be summed up thus: "traditionally, individuals have generally had the right to do as they wish as long as they do not cause unjust harm to another person."

I know there are many examples throughout history that show this has not always been the case. Those are the exceptions that prove the rule. Further, this is a general rule, and I will show examples of the many issues in which this has generally been the case, as you join me on this rebel's journey.

"When people are free to do as they please, they usually imitate each other." —— Eric Hoffer

DRUGS

As I mentioned previously, drug legalization was one of the first issues that helped me down the path towards the ideas of liberty. Growing up in Alabama in the 1980's & 1990's I was taught "drugs are bad." And I remember the "Just say no!" campaign. Like most people, I was taught the government propaganda about drugs, especially the dangers of cannabis as a gateway drug.

In high school, I always knew that I could find drugs, but never felt the urge (or pressure) to do drugs. In fact, I was 32 years old before I ever tried cannabis.

During my public speaking class, someone gave a speech titled "Just Say No is Not Possible." I don't recall any details of that speech and have not actually thought about it in probably 18 years. However, I can't help but guess that in some way the speech helped me accept the truth I would learn just a few years later.

During my senior year government class, the teacher taught us about the failures of alcohol prohibition; yet we were expected to believe that drug prohibition was not only good, but also successful.

Darryl W. Perry

Some time during college, or shortly after, I saw a show on the History Channel about the real history of drugs in America. I was shocked to learn that in the early 1900's not only were cannabis, cocaine & heroin legal, but they could be ordered from the Sear's catalog!

I was astounded to learn that cannabis was made illegal because of racism, yellow journalism and propaganda. Cocaine and heroin were made illegal for similar reasons.

I began to question how one substance (alcohol) required a constitutional amendment to become illegal, yet other substances (cannabis, cocaine & heroin) did not. To this day I have found no sufficient answer other than the federal government during the Nixon Administration essentially forced states to adopt certain drug laws.

Now, over 40 years later, there is some progress being made, at least in some states, in rolling back the Drug War, at least in regards to cannabis. In 2012 voters in Colorado and Washington voted to legalize cannabis, which in reality means that cannabis was to be taxed and regulated.[1] Voters in Oregon, Alaska and Washington DC[2] followed suit in 2014.

Throughout history, until relatively recently, cannabis and other drugs have been completely legal to grow, produce, posses and distribute. While I do not condone the abuse of any substance (tobacco, alcohol, cannabis, cocaine, etc), I do not believe that

---

[1] Taxed and regulated sales began in 2014 in both states. In Colorado, 17 tons of recreational cannabis were sold in 2014, and the state collected approximately $76 million in revenue through taxes and fees. In Washington state, approximately $65 million in tax revenue came in between June 2014 and June 2015. Retailers sold more than 23,000 pounds of cannabis during that period.

[2] Legalization in Washington DC is more akin to a decriminalization measure, since voters were not able to authorize a taxation and regulation structure. Therefore, cannabis can not be legally purchased or sold in the District.

jailing people who use a substance that can be misused is a good way to discourage use or abuse of said substance.

Let's not forget that cannabis does have medicinal qualities, and 23 states currently have laws allowing for medicinal use of cannabis.[3] I have personally found that ingesting cannabis, primarily in the form of a tincture, does help alleviate my chronic headache[4] and joint pain.[5] However, it is difficult for me to find and obtain cannabis in the form I need, so I'm generally forced to suffer without relief. The only other treatment that has helped with the headache is a combination of prescription drugs, which includes a highly addictive barbiturate.

Most people acknowledge that alcohol prohibition was a failure. When will people acknowledge that the War on Drugs is a much costlier failure?

Some people argue that a regulatory structure such as that adopted in Colorado and Washington will be the beginning of the end of the Drug War. While the statistics show that arrests for cannabis possession have declined in Colorado by 84% since 2010, and arrests for distribution of cannabis have declined by 90% in the same time period, arrests for public consumption have risen by over three and a half times in only 1 year (184 in 2013 to 668 in 2014).[6]

---

3   As of July 2015
http://www.ncsl.org/research/health/state-medical-marijuana-laws.aspx

4   As a result of post-concussion syndrome, I've had a headache since 9:45am (Central) August 27, 2011.

5   I've suffered back pain since I was a teenager. In either 2004 or 2005, I fractured my tail bone, which resulted in mild compression of the lower spine. Additionally, I have injured both knees and ankles several times, which has resulted in loss of cartilage in my knees, and symptoms of arthritis.

6   Barry Bard, *Colorado Marijuana Arrests Down 84% Since 2010 as Employment Rate Reaches Six-Year High*, (January 8, 2015),
http://www.marijuana.com/news/2015/01/colorado-marijuana-arrests-down-84-since-2010-as-employment-rate-reaches-six-year-high

However, cannabis is only one aspect of the Drug War. Aside from asset forfeiture, the other aspects of the Drug War are more taboo, and less discussed in any serious manner. Additionally, one must define what is meant by "ending the Drug War." Some would be happy to see only arrests for cannabis possession be eliminated, but would support the continued prosecution of unlicensed sales (regardless if they support licensing sales or not). While others believe that taxing and regulating cannabis, but keeping the "hard stuff" illegal is a good enough end to the Drug War. Yet others believe that all substances should be able to be manufactured, sold, possessed and or consumed without government intervention. I fall in the latter category, and do not believe that taxing and regulating a substance, any substance, can lead to the eventual abolition of that structure of taxation and regulation. I challenge you to think of something, anything, that has had a structure of taxation and regulation removed from it within your life time.

I long for the day in which all substances are as legal as tomatoes. What do I mean? To my knowledge, there are no laws regulating how many tomatoes a person can grow, purchase, sale or posses. There may be laws regulating business activity in general, but not tomatoes specifically. Thus, to truly end the War on Drugs, the federal Controlled Substances Act needs to be repealed, and all state and local laws prohibiting the manufacture, sale, purchase, possession and consumption of all substances must be repealed. By saying this, I am not advocating that anyone consume crystal meth, only that one should not be treated as a criminal for simply doing so. It is not only costly to treat people with vices like criminals, it is also immoral.

TAXATION

The first time I took a "Nolan Chart" quiz was during my senior year of high school. I remember 3 things about that quiz:

1) It was the first time I was aware of different ideological options aside from the standard choices: conservative or liberal; right, left, or center; Republican, Democrat or Independent.

2) I scored "populist" (which is no longer listed on the Nolan Chart) which put me in the lower quadrant near the convergence of the centrist block and the conservative quadrant.

3) The only question I recall was about the rich paying "their fair share" of taxes.

At the time, I said "yes." As the year progressed I learned that the progressive tax structure does tax "the rich" at a higher rate. I never gave a second thought to the fact that there was no tax on income before the ratification of the 16th amendment. And the discussion on taxation was always on the pro's and con's of progressive tax, regressive tax and/or flat tax. During my senior year of high school, I came to like the idea of the flat tax.

In 1999, while working as a traffic reporter for a news/talk radio station, I heard Neal Boortz talk about this new proposal called the "Fair Tax." I was on board, and like the idea of people being able to keep what they earn, and only paying tax when they make a purchase.

It was through Neal Boortz that I heard about the Libertarian Party, the world's smallest political quiz (I took it and scored "conservative libertarian") and the ideas of libertarianism. It was not long before I joined the LP and began learning more about the ideas of libertarianism. A few years later, after moving to Pennsylvania, I ran for Town Supervisor as a Libertarian, and with minimal campaigning, polled 11% in a two-way race against an incumbent Democrat. I had planned to run for State Representative the following year, but was asked to be the LP nominee for State Treasurer. As the LP nominee for State Treasurer, I said I would not write a check the state could not cash, and polled just over 1%, which was higher than the Green Party & Constitution Party candidates combined!

It was around this time that my support for the "Fair Tax" began to fade, and I began to realize that no form of direct taxation is fair.

I do like the idea of user fees, though have not found one that has been implemented by a government that was not carried out in a monopolistic, violent fashion.

There are some people who say that based on the wording of the IRS code the average worker is not required to file a tax return. Some of those people have even gone to jail for failure to file a tax return and/or pay what the IRS claims they owe. Others like to point to statistics similar to the infamous 47% figure that gained notoriety during the 2012 Presidential election, which is the approximate percentage of people who do not pay federal income taxes. Most of the people who mention that statistic, do so in an effort to shame those who don't pay any federal income tax. Every time I hear a statistic like this, I'm reminded of the Whitey

Harrell trial. Mr. Harrell was charged with not filing an Illinois State tax return and was acquitted by the jury. Marcella Brooks, the juror that was vocal in getting the acquittal, recounts in *America: Freedom to Fascism* that the other members of the jury said "but he'll get away with it." Mr. Harrell was acquitted because the jury was not shown the law that proved he was required to file a federal income tax return. Millions of Americans are like the members of that jury – they're not really upset that others aren't paying; they're upset that they are!

I'm not really concerned with whether or not there is a law, statute, regulation, or ordinance in place that says anyone must file a tax return. I'm not concerned, because there are many laws, statutes, regulations, and ordinances in place around the world that attempt to control people, by forcing them to do or not do certain things. In the past, there were laws that said one human could own another human against his will, that if a slave escaped he would be returned to "his master," and that it was illegal to assist a run-away slave. Did those laws make involuntary servitude moral? No, nor did the laws that allowed the Germans to incarcerate and murder anyone of Jewish descent make those acts any less heinous. Just because something is mandated under law does not make it right any more than a law prohibiting something makes it wrong.

The real unanswered question regarding taxes is not "what is someone's fair share?" But rather: Does anyone else own the fruits of your labor? I say, "NO!"

If you support the idea that everyone is equal under the law, then you believe that no person or group has more rights than any other person or group. For instance, I do not have the right to steal your car. Thus, no group – regardless of size – has a right to steal your car; though groups known as government claim such an illegitimate right. They may never steal your car, or they might steal your car under certain circumstances: failure to register with the local DMV; too many citations for driving and/or parking offenses; or simply because your car does not meet some "safety standard." These are not legitimate reasons for the theft of one's transportation. Similarly, governments around the world claim ownership over a portion of your earnings in the form of taxation. If you fail to pay, you risk being thrown in jail and/or possible death. If I attempted to take money from you by force, it would be considered theft or extortion. It is no less theft or extortion when government does it!

Knowing that taxation is theft, or at the very least extortion, how can a government operate absent this method of getting money? I believe that governments (if they are to continue existing) can operate without taxation in a similar way that your neighborhood grocer operates without taxation. Any proposed government project should be able to be funded through voluntary means. Just as your local grocer doesn't point (or threaten to point) a gun to your head to force you to purchase his groceries; governments should not use the same tactics to force you to fund its schools, roads, post offices, bureaucrats, regulatory agencies, military conquests, and/or any other government function.

This does not mean that I oppose schools, roads, and post offices. In fact, I like all three of those things, and regularly use two of them. I'm opposed to the use of force to fund them. I've been a regular contributor to the arts and libraries, however I'm opposed to the use of force to fund them!

For a quick comparison between the private sector and government monopoly, lets look at the delivery of mail and packages. During the fiscal year ending in September 2012, the

A Rebel's Journey

United States Post Office had a deficit of $15.9 billion[7], while UPS was expecting profits to be over $5 billion in 2014.[8]

With regards to education, some statistics show that government-funded schools spend one and a half times more per student than their privately run counterparts.[9] Private schools also hire more teachers and spend much less on administration than government-funded schools. Many museums operate almost entirely on private-funding, yet claim they will cease to exist absent the government funds they do receive. There are also free-market solutions to policing and roads that currently exist, and operate better than the one-size-fits-all government-controlled solutions.

I admit that I do not have all of the answers, though I do offer solutions. My solution to operating a government without taxation is to have said government (if such would even exist in a libertarian society) rely on voluntary contributions, just as privately run businesses and charities do!

7   Ron Nixon, *Postal Service Reports Loss of $15 Billion*, (November 15, 2012),
http://www.nytimes.com/2012/11/16/us/politics/postal-service-reports-a-nearly-16-billion-loss.html

8   *UPS Says Profits for Us, Concessions for You*,
http://makeupsdeliver.org/ups-says-profits-for-us-concessions-for-you/

9   Andrew J. Coulson *Private Schools Now 33% Off!*, (October 18, 2006),
http://www.cato.org/blog/private-schools-now-33

"Freedom is not worth having if it does not include the freedom to make mistakes." —Mahatma Gandhi

BUY LOCAL

When I was younger it was, and to some extent it still is to this day, a fad to "Buy American." I recall that being one of the draws of Walmart when Sam Walton was running the company. Even in my early teens, Ross Perot talked about "the giant sucking sound" during his first Presidential campaign. I even recall in my early twenties being upset that it was difficult to find cheap products that weren't labeled "Made in China." It didn't seem to matter to me that the products from other countries were made better, I was taught that outsourcing jobs was killing the American economy. Until my late 20's or early 30's I never asked the question: why are companies outsourcing jobs?

The simple answer is "cheaper labor." But why is the labor cheaper in other countries? Those who oppose a global economy, like Perot, say "South of the border, [you] pay a dollar an hour for labor,...have no health care—that's the most expensive single element in making a car— have no environmental controls, no pollution controls and no retirement, and you don't care about anything but making money, there will be a giant sucking sound going south."

I can sum up Perot's answer with the words: regulations and taxes. The Competitive Enterprise Institute calculates that compliance with federal regulations costs Americans $1.863

trillion for 2013[10]; and tax compliance costs an estimated $1 trillion annually in addition to the taxes that are paid, according to the Mercatus Center[11]! Put into perspective, compliance with taxes and regulations cost the average household $23,011 per year. The CEI reports, "This exceeds every item in the household budget except housing – more than health care, food, transportation, entertainment, apparel, services, and savings." This explains a lot about why companies export jobs. But what of the people who are opposed to companies doing what companies are expected to do: make a profit!?!

I recently read a pair of articles that on the surface are only tangentially connected. However after a little deep thought, I realized the authors are looking at the same problem from both a micro and macro level. Again, after some thought I came up with the hypothesis: people who are xenophobic have a flawed understanding of economics.

Nikki Burgess, from Students for Liberty, writes[12], "Let's begin with a basic economic principle: The more people an economy has, the more productive it can be. This appeals to common sense—given equal circumstances, 20 people working will create value more than 10." For the sake of argument it doesn't matter whether the 20 people live in one community or not. Those who oppose trade and/or immigration will argue that there may not be enough work for 20 people, and that some of the new people will work for less, thus putting someone out of a job. While that may be true in the short term, it is not true in the long term.

---

10   Clyde Wayne Crews, *Ten Thousand Commandments 2014*, (April 29, 2014),
https://cei.org/studies/ten-thousand-commandments-2014

11   Jason J. Fichtner, Jacob Feldman, *The Hidden Cost of Tax Compliance*, (May 20, 2013),
http://mercatus.org/publication/hidden-costs-tax-compliance

12   Nikki Burgess, *The Economic Case for Open Borders*, (December 16, 2014),
http://studentsforliberty.org/blog/2014/12/16/open-border-economics

A Rebel's Journey

Burgess adds, "Economists agree that immigrants complement, rather than compete with, the native work force. Even assuming the opposite—that migrants and natives do compete for the same work—the estimated net benefit to natives from migrant labor is still $22 billion annually... Besides, competition is good; it ensures that the most productive candidates are employed and it makes goods cheaper by driving down production costs. However, empirically, immigrants and natives do not usually pursue the same work."

On the macro level, Brian Brenberg & Chris Horst write[13], "History and research show that as trade increases, poverty decreases, and China is a prime example. Since 1978, when the country opened to foreign investment, China has grown to become the world's largest trader - measured by total imports and exports. The results have been striking.

In 2012 alone, average factory wages in China rose 14 percent. In manufacturing, specifically, worker wages have increased 71 percent since 2008. Over the last thirty years, Chinese families living in extreme poverty dropped from 84 percent to under 10 percent."

Of course, China is just one example of the benefits of trade. A report released in 2011 by Yale University and the Brookings Institution[14] found that the world's population living below the extreme poverty line plummeted from 52 percent to 15 percent in just 30 years from 1981 to 2011. Globalization and the spread of freer markets were credited with "enabl[ing] the developing world to begin converging on advanced economy incomes after centuries of divergence."

---

13   Brian Brenberg & Chris Horst, *'Buy Local' Is Really Bad Economics*, (December 30, 2014),
http://www.realclearmarkets.com/articles/2014/12/30/buy_local_is_really_bad_economics_101460.html
14   Laurence Chandy, Geoffrey Gertz, Yale Global, *With Little Notice, Globalization Reduced Poverty*, (July 5, 2011),
http://yaleglobal.yale.edu/content/little-notice-globalization-reduced-poverty

Darryl W. Perry

Aside from being bad economics, xenophobia is also irrational. Advocates of "Buy Local" use slogans like "Don't buy from strangers, buy from neighbors." This may make people in small towns feel good, when they buy from the Mom & Pop stores, however one needs to look deeper. Chances are the products in the Mom & Pop store were brought in from somewhere, which means there was most likely trade with someone outside the community (i.e. a stranger). This is not a bad thing. The numbers don't lie, when trade happens wealth spreads, and when wealth spreads everybody wins by becoming less poor!

IMMIGRATION

Like the other issues discussed in this book, immigration is an issue in which my search for traditional values lead me to conclude that people should be allowed to decide for themselves where they live, regardless of where they were born.

In school, I was taught about the hard working immigrants who helped build the transcontinental railroad, the plight of immigrants in the slums of New York, and about the immigrants who spent the last of what they had to come to the United States because America was the "Land of Opportunity." I was told about the millions of immigrants who came through Ellis Island, being greeted by the Statue of Liberty, because they knew they could make a better life in a country with more freedoms.

However, I was never taught that there were no federal laws regulating immigration[15] until the passage of the Page Act of 1875, which was introduced to "end the danger of cheap Chinese labor and immoral Chinese women." A few years later, the Chinese Exclusion Act was passed, which among other things prohibited all immigration of Chinese laborers. The Bureau of Immigration, which operated the Ellis Island Immigration Station

---

15 The United States Naturalization Law of March 26, 1790 limited naturalization (i.e. citizenship) to immigrants who were free white persons of good character. American Indians, indentured servants, slaves, free blacks, and Asians were prevented from obtaining citizenship under this law, but were not prevented from immigrating.

was not created until 1891, the year before Ellis Island became the place that nearly 12 million immigrants were processed.

Also, like most people, I never thought a lot about the subject for most of my life. Then in late 1999 and early 2000 the story of Elián González made national headlines. Young Elián's mother drowned in November 1999 while attempting to flee Cuba with her boyfriend, son, and 11 others. During the trek from Cuba to the United States, the boat they were on sank, and only Elián and two other people survived, floating in inner tubes until they were rescued by two fishermen, who turned them over to the U.S. Coast Guard. INS placed Elián in the custody of his paternal great-uncle in Miami, Florida. The situation sparked a national debate with conservatives like Rush Limbaugh saying the boy should stay in the United States with his family, and the Clinton Administration saying the boy should be returned to his father in Cuba. During the entire debate, I kept asking the question (to which no one seemed to know answer): What does the law say should happen?

Several years later, during national protests for immigrants rights, I asked the question: If these people protesting are here illegally, why are they not arrested? And advocated the position that people wishing to come to the country should simply follow the laws. It was around this time that I began trying to find out the laws. I learned about the quota systems, and the outrageous fees required for people to move to the supposed Land of the Free. While working for an airline, I worked with an immigrant from Malawi, who told me about the tens of thousands of dollars in fees he'd paid in the previous 8 years, and he was still going through the immigration process. Finally, immigration had become personal. As an aside, I've concluded that most people only change their opinion of an issue when it becomes personal.

A Rebel's Journey

While working for the airline, I was able to take advantage of flight benefits. I was able to travel, visit historical sites, and learn. One of the first trips I took was to Key West, Florida. While walking around the island, I learned that just months prior to my visit, someone from the city had attempted to annex an abandoned portion of the Seven Mile Bridge. This was done in protest of the official US policy that the Cuban immigrants on the bridge still had "wet feet" under the "wet feet, dry feet policy" as it applied to Cuban immigrants. This act, while not officially recognized, showed an amazing act of kindness and compassion, and again caused me to question my position. A trip a few months later to Ellis Island, was the tipping point in causing me to completely change my position. For it was there, in New York that I learned of the history of immigration laws in the United States, and of the blatant racism that was the rationale behind so many of the laws restricting and/or prohibiting immigration into the United States.

During my tenure on the National Committee of the Boston Tea Party, the Party adopted a program plank[16] stating:

> **End the Immigration Fiasco**: Rather than suddenly decide to enforce long-ignored immigration laws, the United States should open the borders to trade and travel. We should loosen restrictions on citizens and visitors alike, allowing people of many backgrounds and cultures to coexist in a society of social and economic freedom and prosperity. The Immigration and Customs Enforcement and Border Patrol agencies at all levels of government should be abolished and dismantled immediately.

Current federal immigration laws are convoluted and give preferential treatment to individuals from certain countries, it

16   The Boston Tea Party had a platform that could not be modified, as such the Party adopted a 5 plank Program every two years.

relies on quotas, hosts and in some cases an immigration lottery, as well as preferred treatment to athletes and refugees. This must change, and there should be one uniform immigration law. I believe the best law to work with, is the "wet foot, dry foot rule" in place for people fleeing Cuba. Under this rule, anyone from Cuba who makes it safely into the United States, is allowed to stay However, the aspect of this rule that I don't like is that the Coast Guard patrols the waters looking for people with "wet feet" in order to redirect them back to Cuba.

As a supporter of voluntary human interaction, I believe that people should be able to travel, live, and work wherever they wish. This includes the right of people to move from the country in which they were born to another country without the need to jump through legislative hoops and hurdles. The immigration policy of the United States of America should once again resemble the words written on the Statue of Liberty:

"Give me your tired, your poor,
Your huddled masses yearning to breathe free,
The wretched refuse of your teeming shore.
Send these, the homeless, tempest-tost to me,
I lift my lamp beside the golden door!"

DEATH PENALTY

As a teenager, as I was forming opinions on various issues, I supported the death penalty. I supported it because I believed what I was told:

- Death penalty is a deterrent
- Death penalty saves money
- It's the Christian thing to do[17]
- An eye for an eye, a life for a life/the punishment fits the crime

I have always heard that "the death penalty is a deterrent" without any real evidence to back up the claim, and for many years I believed it. That was until I did my own research. Some people claim that the death penalty isn't meant to deter society-at-large from killing, but that it prevents the actual murderer from killing more victims. Naci Mocan, an economics professor at the University of Colorado at Denver who co-authored a 2003 study, and a 2006 study that re-examined the data, said, "Science does really draw a conclusion. It did. There is no question about it. The conclusion is there is a deterrent effect." He found that each execution results in five fewer homicides, and commuting a death sentence means five more homicides. This of course, assumes that

17   Genesis 9:6 "Whoever sheds man's blood, his blood shall be shed by man. For He made man in the image of God."
Exodus 21:12 "He that strikes a man so that he dies, dying he shall die."

everyone who kills one person is a would-be serial killer, out for blood. This study also seems to be at odds with other more empirical data which not only shows murder rates per 100,000 having dropped by 50% over the last 20 years, but also that the murder rates in states *with* the death penalty are an average of 22% higher than that of states without the death penalty.[18] If the death penalty is a deterrent, why are the murder rates higher in states where murderers are executed?

It's possible that at one time, the death penalty may have saved money; however, the figures I've been able to find do not support this claim. A report from 2011, shows that it costs California taxpayers $90,000 per year more to incarcerate an inmate on death row, as compared to an inmate in general population serving a sentence of life without the possibility of parole. This additional costs is due to a couple of factors: mandatory appeals, and what amounts to solitary confinement. There are also the costs of carrying out the execution, often times many years after the conviction – I'll touch on this in more detail later. While the data shows that the death penalty is more expensive than life without parole; cost should not be a determining factor in whether or not something is moral or ethical.

This brings me to the final two points that I once believed. While it's true that certain Bible passages do mention execution as being punishment for certain offenses, it also states "You shall keep far away from a false matter. And do not kill the innocent and the righteous; for I will not justify the wicked."[19] "Do not kill the innocent!" This passage seems to have passed by some death penalty advocates who claim the Bible as their guide.

---

18   Death Penalty Information Center, *Deterrence: States Without the Death Penalty Have Had Consistently Lower Murder Rates,*
http://www.deathpenaltyinfo.org/deterrence-states-without-death-penalty-have-had-consistently-lower-murder-rates
19   Exodus 23:7

A Rebel's Journey

Since September 2014, there have been at least 7 people exonerated from death row who had been incarcerated for at least 25 years.

- In September 2014, Henry McCollum and Leon Brown, brothers, were freed after 30 years because of evidence uncovered by the North Carolina Innocence Inquiry Commission. The Death Penalty Information Center reports, "both men are intellectually disabled – McCollum has an IQ in the 60s and Brown has scored as low as 49 on IQ tests. They have maintained their innocence since their trial, saying they were unaware they were signing a confession."

- In November 2014, Ricky Jackson, Wiley Bridgeman, and Kwame Ajamu were exonerated 39 years after their convictions, after the lone witness in their case recanted and said that he did not in fact witness the crime; there was no other evidence linking the three men to the murder.

- In March 2015, Debra Milke had all charges from her 1990 conviction dismissed as a result of "egregious" police and prosecutorial misconduct.

- In April 2015, Anthony Hinton had the charges against him for 2 murders committed in 1985 dismissed after experts said they could not link the bullets to a gun found in his home when he was arrested.

According to the Death Penalty Information Center, there have been 152 people exonerated from death row since 1973.[20] Twenty of those individuals were exonerated because of DNA evidence, meaning the other 132 people to be exonerated from death row had been convicted because of false confessions, unreliable witnesses, police misconduct, faulty evidence, etc. This

20   Death Penalty Information Center, *Innocence: List of Those Freed From Death Row*, http://www.deathpenaltyinfo.org/innocence-list-those-freed-death-row

alone should raise some questions not only about the use of the death penalty as a means of punishment, but about the accuracy of the entire justice system. But I digress. Considering that over 1,400 people have been executed since 1973, and 152 people have been exonerated in that same time period, it is probable that innocent people have been executed in the name of justice. If only 1 innocent person has been executed for a crime they did not commit, that should be enough to oppose state-funded executions; because state-funded executions use tax-payer dollars to carry out a punishment that some find objectionable. To paraphrase a quote from Thomas Jefferson: it is sinful and tyrannical to force someone to pay for something they abhor!

However, is it really justice to carry out a punishment years after an offense was committed? One maxim of common law is "justice delayed is justice denied." I contend that such delayed punishment, as we see in cases of those on death row, is in fact cruel and unusual punishment, and I dare say: torture. It forces the person, who may or may not have committed the crime, to wonder "is today the day I find out when I die?" Just as it would be considered cruel and unusual to punish a 35 year old man for an offense he committed when he was 5 years old, it should be equally cruel and unusual to withhold punishment for some length of time after a conviction. If justice is the goal of capital punishment, then a delayed punishment can not be construed to be justice! Again, I point to the likelihood of innocent people being executed, the Death Penalty Information Center lists 25 people as either executed but possibly innocent or as having been posthumously pardoned, in one case the pardon came 94 years after execution. It is statistically probable that other innocent people have been executed, and that makes state-funded capital punishment immoral![21]

---

21 What then of private capital punishment? I believe it could be moral (based on the eye-for-an-eye version of morality); if, and only if, the person committing the

MARRIAGE EQUALITY

When I was younger, and much more conservative, the debate surrounding marriage wasn't whether or not same-sex couples should be able to get legally married; rather whether or not people should be allowed to easily get a divorce. It wasn't until my high school years that same-sex marriage was really a topic of discussion. At the time because I had been taught that God said marriage is one man and one woman, I was opposed to the idea of same-sex marriage. Again, it was my search for the meaning of traditional values that lead me to conclude otherwise.

As I mentioned previously, I went to church regularly as a teenager, and even though there are several prominent figures in the Bible who had multiple wives, I was taught in church that was an oddity, and a sin; and, since laws are supposedly based upon a moral code, anything sinful is supposed to be illegal. The thought process goes like this: the Old Testament says homosexuality is a sin, therefore same-sex marriage should be illegal. The Old Testament also says that wearing a garment of mixed cloth is a sin, but it's perfectly legal for two people who wear cotton/wool blend clothing to get married, as it is for people who eat seafood, or grow multiple crops in the same field. Growing up, I was never

---

vigilante act had proof well beyond reasonable doubt – I dare say 110% proof (i.e. caught the person in the act of a murder/attempted murder, or rape) – AND did not unreasonably delay the carrying out of justice.

taught the fact that government involvement in marriage is a recent development in human civilization, or that the reasons for the first marriage licenses in the United States were to prevent interracial marriages.

Even as an adult in 2006, my position on marriage was evolving. At the time, I knew some of the history of marriage licensing laws, and would have preferred government not be involved, but thought "as long as government is involved, we should use the traditional definition," and begrudgingly, I voted for what became Amendment 774[22][23] of the Alabama Constitution, to this day it is the only vote I've cast that I regret. I regret it, because I cast a vote in ignorance. While I had been taught that marriage was traditionally one man and one woman, that was incorrect. Until recently, consensual polygamy was a fairly common and accepted practice, and is still common in some parts of the world. Which meant that marriage could be a man and multiple women, a woman and multiple men or multiple men and

22　(a) This amendment shall be known and may be cited as the Sanctity of Marriage Amendment.

(b) Marriage is inherently a unique relationship between a man and a woman. As a matter of public policy, this state has a special interest in encouraging, supporting, and protecting this unique relationship in order to promote, among other goals, the stability and welfare of society and its children. A marriage contracted between individuals of the same sex is invalid in this state.

(c) Marriage is a sacred covenant, solemnized between a man and a woman, which, when the legal capacity and consent of both parties is present, establishes their relationship as husband and wife, and which is recognized by the state as a civil contract.

(d) No marriage license shall be issued in the State of Alabama to parties of the same sex.

(e) The State of Alabama shall not recognize as valid any marriage of parties of the same sex that occurred or was alleged to have occurred as a result of the law of any jurisdiction regardless of whether a marriage license was issued.

(f) The State of Alabama shall not recognize as valid any common law marriage of parties of the same sex.

(g) A union replicating marriage of or between persons of the same sex in the State of Alabama or in any other jurisdiction shall be considered and treated in all respects as having no legal force or effect in this state and shall not be recognized by this state as a marriage or other union replicating marriage.

23　This amendment was ruled unconstitutional on January 23, 2015 in the case of *Searcy v. Strange*.

multiple women. So, the position I had been taught as a child was both historically inaccurate, and based on the premise that you can legislate morality, something many conservatives try to do while picking and choosing which aspects to enforce.

Daniel Waechter of Privatize Marriage writes, "marriage licenses have only existed on any significant scale since 1929. No one in the US before that was required to have a marriage license in order to practice their fundamental right to marry."

The fundamental right to marry. Fundamental rights are not something that should be regulated or licensed. Historically marriage has been handled by churches, not government. Nowadays with more people identifying as non-religious, absent government involvement, there would certainly be secular entities willing to solemnize a marriage. Jesse Kline of the National Post writes[24], "the central question... is whether the state should be dictating the domestic arrangements of consenting adults." Now, with an informed opinion, I say loudly: "NO!" If any number of consenting adults wish to get married, they should be allowed to do so, as long as the relationship remains consensual. If two people wish to get married, and either partner wishes to bring another person into the relationship, they should legally be allowed to do so, as long as the relationship remains consensual.

What then of marriage licensing? A fundamental right, such as the right to marry, is not something that should be regulated or licensed. In other words: get government out of the marriage business!

Getting government out of the business of issuing – and in most case requiring – a marriage license will be a challenge

---

24   Jesse Kline, *Jesse Kline on polygamy: State shouldn't interfere in consensual adult relationships*, (November 24, 2011),

http://news.nationalpost.com/full-comment/jesse-kline-on-polygamy-state-shouldnt-interfere-in-consensual-adult-relationships because government doesn't like giving up power it has, nor does government like losing revenue sources once obtained. Providing marriage licenses is big business for the state. On average, 2.3 million couples are married per year in the United States, with the average marriage license costing $33.74; that provides a steady stream of income (roughly $77.6 million) for those who want control over your life.

People have become too accepting of government licensing and regulation. If you don't want government regulating who you can share Thanksgiving dinner with, if/where you attend church or who you can date; why then are you willing to accept regulations on your committed relationships?

FOREIGN AFFAIRS

For most people, American foreign policy began on September 11, 2001. In some ways, I fit into this category, and in other ways I did not. I'll explain. When I was young, maybe 9 or 10 years old, I vaguely recall hearing some of the news about the Iran-Iraq conflict, and vaguely recall the Iran-contra scandal, though never really understood what the issues were. I recall watching the Berlin Wall collapse, and being told that America had won the Cold War, but never really understood what the Cold War was. Then in 1991, George H.W. Bush sent troops into Kuwait to defend the tiny gulf nation from the Iraqi military. Several years later, Bill Clinton sent the military (under NATO command) to fight in what was essentially a civil war in Yugoslavia, and the US military for reasons still unknown bombed an aspirin factory.

As a teenager, I was taught to respect those who served in the military, and was told "without them, we'd be speaking German right now," and "people died for your freedom." Because I didn't know any better, I believed the things I was told. As a Senior in high school because of my high score on the ASVAB[25], I was recruited heavily by the US Navy to become a nuclear engineer on a submarine. I was also recruited by the Marines, and preferred

---

25   Armed Services Vocational Aptitude Battery

the possibility of working at a US Embassy to living in a tiny metal tube. I signed preliminary paperwork with the US Marines in March 1996. However, after much prayer for God's guidance in my decision, I became a conscientious objector[26].

I was also taught about Switzerland, and that one reason they weren't involved in either World War was because of their official position of remaining neutral, and being an isolationist country[27]. I remember saying several times to my friends, "there's a lot to be said for being an isolationist country, look at Switzerland."

Then on that Tuesday in September 2001, everything changed. For the first time since 1941, America was attacked by an outside entity. My initial response after the shock wore off, was that the military should carpet bomb the entire Middle East back into the stone age. After all "they" attacked "us" first.

A few months later, I began to think, logically and rationally. If 19 people hijacked airplanes and flew them into buildings, then the guilty people are dead. There is no need to kill more innocent people. While I did not support the invasion of Iraq in 2003, I was not necessarily opposed to it either – partly because I didn't want to be seen as supporting the terrorists[28]. We knew that Saddam Hussein was a bad guy, right? Why was there the need to falsely claim that he possessed weapons of mass destruction? After George W. Bush's "Mission Accomplished" moment, and the US military remained in Iraq, I was convinced that invading was the wrong thing to do. If you order a pizza, the delivery guy leaves after delivering the pizza; he doesn't stay to help you eat it. Furthermore, there was no official declaration of war to invade

---

26   Merriam-Webster
http://www.merriam-webster.com/dictionary/conscientious+objector

27   Switzerland should properly be called a non-interventionist country.

28   On September 5, 2001, President George W. Bush said, "either you're with us or you're the terrorists." This was relayed in the media that anyone who opposed the war, was a terrorist, or at the very least a terrorist-sympathizer.

Iraq, or Afghanistan for that matter, which makes the war even more illegal – more on that later.

What I would later find out is that American foreign policy, especially the interventionist foreign policy in the Middle East, began long before September 2001, or even the Iran-Iraq conflict of the 1980's.

The US government, either covertly or overtly, supported at least three successful coups in the Middle East between 1949 and 1963, as well as several that were unsuccessful. Not to mention the support to undermine or weaken the governments of several Middle Eastern countries; or the support of Afghani freedom fighters to expel the Soviet invasion; or the sanctions imposed against the governments of Iran and Iraq; or the aid to the Israeli military in the form of money and weapons, which in part has been used to oppress the Palestinians. In short, for 50+ years before September 11, 2001, the government of the United States was intervening in the Middle East, and for 10 years before, the US military was bombing Iraq, and building bases. In 2007, Ron Paul said, "What would we say here if China was doing this in our country or in the Gulf of Mexico? We would be objecting. We need to look at what we do from the perspective of what would happen if somebody else did it to us."[29]

Some people say that anyone who says blowback is the reason for 9/11 is "blaming America for 9/11." Which is absurd. Explaining why someone responded in a certain manner is not the same as condoning the response.

Between late 2004 and early 2007, I was still in a transition phase. The "Mission Accomplished" moment had persuaded me that the Iraq invasion was wrong. The Afghan government saw its first direct election; democracy was one of the goals of the War on

29   Llewellyn H. Rockwell Jr., *Ron Paul on Blowback*, (May 17, 2007),
https://mises.org/library/ron-paul-blowback

Terror, right? And I finally began looking at the actual cost of the fighting. Not just the monetary costs, which in 2006 was over $400 billion, but also the human cost: approximately 60,000 civilians in Iraq, and upwards of 28,000 Afghan civilians, not including the thousand of military personnel who were killed as a result of the fighting. By late 2007, the "I support the troops" magnet was off my vehicle. By late 2008, there was a "War Is Not The Answer" sticker in its place.

My anti-war position was only strengthened after Private Manning revealed information exposing possible war crimes in 2010. During a pretrial conference on February 28, 2013, Manning, reading from a prepared statement, said there was no pressure by WikiLeaks to release the information, that *The Washington Post*, *The New York Times*, and *Reuters* had been approached with the documents, but they did not want what was being offered. Manning admitted to being "upset" or "disturbed" by the leaked information, but that it did not contain anything that would harm the United States if it became public.

Regarding the so called Collateral Murder video, Manning said the "most alarming part to me was the seemingly delightful bloodlust," and that those in the video "seemed to not value human life by referring to them as 'dead bastards.'"

Manning added, "I was disturbed by the response to injured children... I wanted the American public to know that not everyone in Iraq and Afghanistan was a target that needed to be engaged and neutralized." And concluded "I believe that if the general public ... had access to the information ... this could spark a domestic debate as to the role of the military and foreign policy in general," and "I felt I accomplished something that would allow me to have a clear conscience."

A Rebel's Journey

For this act of courage, and being a whistleblower *is* an act of courage, Private Manning was sentenced to 35 years in prison. And unfortunately, the domestic debate that Private Manning hoped to spark, seems to have never really begun.

I have come full circle, back to a non-interventionist position. There is a misconception among many people that those who support a foreign policy of non-intervention are the same as those supporting isolationism. Not only is this assumption incorrect, it is based on ignorance and years of misinformation. While isolationists are, by definition, non-interventionists, they're also ardent nationalists, or protectionists.

Isolationism is properly defined as a foreign policy which combines abstention from alliances and other international intervention (non-interventionism) and economic relations (protectionism).[30] It asserts both of the following:

1. Non-interventionism – the refusal to become involved in another country's business, problems, etc.[31]
2. Protectionism – a policy of government economic protection for domestic producers through restrictions on foreign competitors.[32]

The key difference between isolationism and non-interventionism (or interventionists, for that matter) is that most everyone practices non-interventionism in his/her private life. How can I be sure that most people practice non-intervention in their private life? It's actually quite easy. The principle of non-intervention is related to the non-aggression axiom, which states "that it shall be legal for anyone to do anything he wants, provided only that he not initiate (or threaten) violence against the

30   Merriam-Webster
http://www.merriam-webster.com/dictionary/isolationism
31   Merriam-Webster
http://www.merriam-webster.com/dictionary/nonintervention
32   Merriam-Webster
http://www.merriam-webster.com/dictionary/protectionism

Darryl W. Perry

person or legitimately owned property of another." Most everyone gets through the day without interfering in the life of other people. Sure, you interact with people, this is the individual equivalent of international free-trade. However, you rarely, if ever, involve yourself in the disputes of other people, unless the dispute involves a friend, loved one, or someone that asks for your assistance. This is the individual equivalent to the philosophy proposed by Thomas Jefferson, "Peace, commerce and honest friendship with all nations--entangling alliances with none."

In *Inclined to Liberty*[33] Louis Carabini explains the small group/large group fallacy:

> "in a small setting, it is easy to envision all the effects of an action, thereby giving a proposal a more accurate evaluation. Reasoning and common sense (intuition) can be valuable tools when predicting the outcome of a proposed policy or event within a small group. However, such tools become far less reliable when assessing outcomes in larger groups. When we interact with others in small groups, our instincts, for the most part, tell us without much deliberation, that we can achieve our goals with less effort and conflict when the means to those goals align with 'the Golden Rule.' In a family, neighborhood, company, business relationship, or similar small group, most of us will adopt 'the Golden Rule' as our guide. However, we tend to abandon that concept when it comes to a large political group."

---

33   Louis E. Caribini, *Inclined to Liberty*, (Auburn: Ludwig von Mises Institute, 2008), 27

If non-intervention is not only practiced, but welcomed by individuals and small groups of people; why should it not be practiced by the nation as a whole?

"When a man is denied the right to live the life he believes in, he has no choice but to become an outlaw." —— Nelson Mandela

DEMOCRACY

One of the first things I did upon turning 18, after signing up for Selective Service, was register to vote. I was eager to be able to partake in the electoral process, it didn't matter that the primary election was 4 months away, I wanted to be able to say: "I'm now an eligible voter!"

I had been taught that democracy was one of the cornerstones of the American republic, and that voting was a way in which I could let my voice be heard. Never-mind the fact that my voice was an anonymous mark on a piece of paper that was thrown together with the voices of millions of other people, and only a single voice would ultimately be heard; I wanted to make my uninformed voice heard. Not only would I learn that my voice is often not heard, because I don't vote for winning candidates, but because decisions are generally not made in a democratic manner. Policy, for the most part, is not made at the ballot box; rather policy is made by men and women in legislative buildings claiming to represent the people. Not satisfied with simply casting a ballot and not seeing the results I preferred, I was told by a few people that the only way to actually change things is to run for office.

The first time I ran for public office was in 2003 in Donegal Township, Pennsylvania. I collected 10 signatures to run for

Darryl W. Perry

Township Supervisor – the equivalent of City Councilor – as the only opposition to the incumbent. During the first interview I had with a local newspaper, I was asked "Why are you running as a Libertarian?" I had been a Libertarian for about 4 years at the time, and never considered running as anything else, nor did I consider that I'd ever be asked why I was affiliated with my party of choice, and responded, "Are you asking the incumbent why he's running as a Democrat?" He replied that he'd never considered asking that question to a Republican or Democrat, and pushed for an answer. I gave an answer about not feeling represented by the two established parties, and believing in limited government. Ultimately, I spent $30 campaigning and received 11% of the vote. None of the issues I raised during the campaign were ever acted upon, and my voice was ultimately ignored. That however, did not discourage me from running other campaigns, again bringing issues to the table that weren't otherwise being discussed. Expanding the debate, and spreading a message are two of the reasons I'm waging a Presidential campaign in 2016.

I still remember being taught in 8th grade American history that the electoral system of the United States was a combination of majority rule and minority right. However, as I read and studied history, I found out that the right of the minority was often discarded for the benefit of the majority. One could certainly look through American history and note the instances where the rights of a minority were infringed "for the greater good."

- Internment of Japanese Americans during World War 2
- Chattel slavery
- Forced segregation
- Relocation of Native Americans

To paraphrase Ayn Rand, the individual is the smallest minority, if the rights of anyone are infringed, you can't claim to protect minority right. What does that mean? If you believe that no person has more rights than any other person, then no group of people can have more rights than any person, because a person can't grant rights to another that they do not possess themselves. Since no group of people can have more rights than any individual member of the group, no group can revoke the rights of any other person or group. Therefore, any law, regulation, statute, or other dictate can not rightly infringe on the rights of any person. Yet that is exactly what happens in a democracy, whether it be direct democracy or a representative democracy.

In practical application, democracy is a system in which a plurality of people who show up on voting day attempt to impose their will on everyone else. Allow me to pause for a second to say that I'm not opposed to voting, as I believe one can vote in self-defense[34]; I am however opposed to the system that uses threats of force to make everyone in a geographic area comply with the wishes of a few. If the joint opinion of the plurality changes in the middle of the term, in most cases there is no option for recourse.

Why then should people not have a manner in which they can let it be known that they do not consent to the ideas expressed by the local (or national) government? Why must everyone be obligated to live under the policies chosen by a plurality of people as expressed on a given day?

The idea seems foreign to most people, and they would likely claim "it would never work," or "it's never been done before." Both claims are, in fact, false! Polycentric societies have existed in several places at various times throughout history; in Medina during the time of the Muslim Prophet Muhammad, in Gaelic areas during the middle ages, and to a lesser extent in the United

---

34   Examples of voting in self-defense: voting for a tax decrease; voting to repeal a regulation or law; voting for a candidate who will limit the size, scope or power of a government entity.

States before the New Deal when most people received social services from fraternal organizations or mutual aid societies.

I long for the day when democracy, much like slavery, is viewed not only as a thing of the past but also a system that should have never existed. I recall being taught that governments exist with the consent of the governed; it's even stated in the Declaration of Independence. Therefore, no government or society should be able to claim a monopoly over any geographic area, and every individual should be able to give his consent to and/or withdraw his consent from any government at any time. At present, can someone choose to not consent? If not, how is this forced consent any different than a contract signed under duress?

EDUCATION

"I have never let my schooling interfere with my
education." ~ Mark Twain

I began my schooling by attending kindergarten and first
grade at private schools, before our family moved to a nearby
town where I was enrolled in the public school system from
which I graduated. I could tell at that young age that something
wasn't quite right, because things I began learning in first grade –
specifically cursive handwriting – I wasn't being taught until near
the end of second grade at the new school. I would later find out
that government-funded public schooling was a recent
development in society. The government-run school system we
know today began in Prussia in the late 18th century, and was
brought to the United States by Horace Mann, then secretary of
the Massachusetts Board of Education, who toured German
schools in 1843, and brought those ideas back to the United
States.[35] Mary Ruwart wrote in *Healing Our World*[36]:

"Early in our country's history, Americans were
considered to be among the most literate people
in the world. Schooling was neither compulsory

---

35   Michiel Visser, *Public education versus liberty: The pedigree of an idea*, (March 27,
     2008),
http://www.schoolandstate.org/Knowledge/Visser-PEvsLiberty.htm
36   Mary Ruwart, *Healing Our World: The Other Piece of the Puzzle*, (Kalamazoo:
     SunStar Press, 1993), 127

nor free, although private 'charity' schools provided education to those too poor to afford formal instruction. Licensing requirements for teachers and schools were almost non-existent...

The diverse education available in the United States greatly pleased the immigrants, who came from societies where their children could not go to a school that taught the values they cherished. Some influential citizens, however, felt that society was disrupted, rather than enriched, by the different perspectives and faiths that the immigrants brought with them. With a uniform system of 'American' education, they could mold children into what they perceived as proper citizens."

Public schools do NOT exist to educate children, rather these schools exist to mold children into replicas of one another.

One young man with a vision of breaking that mold is a young man by the name of Erik Finman. In 2014 it came to light that he made a six-figure profit on a bitcoin investment, and then opened his own business. In 2012, Finman received $1,000 from his grandmother and invested it in bitcoin. Nearly 18 months later, he sold his investment for $100,000 "and used the earnings to launch Botangle.com, an online tutoring service that runs on video chat."[37]

In a Reddit AMA[38], he said, "I'm Erik Finman, a 15-year old entrepreneur from Idaho... I owe a lot to my older brother. He told me about Bitcoins and help me get set up with 0.2 bitcoins that he

---

37   Samantha Murphy Kelly, *15-year-old makes $100,000 on Bitcoin, launches startup*, (June 10, 2014),
http://mashable.com/2014/06/10/botangle/
38   AMA stands for Ask Me Anything
http://www.reddit.com/r/Entrepreneur/comments/25u81a/im_15_and_i_have_20_people_working_for_me_all

gave me. And my grandmother just out of the blue gave me a $1000 check for Easter... And I just said screw it, let's buy bitcoins with this money so I can trump my brother in how many bitcoins he had at the time." Adding, "With my earnings I decided to address some of the negative experiences I had in the educational system. Tutoring that is focused and student-centric and engages students in ways responsive to needs and available technology became my passion."

Finman said he didn't think of Botangle as a company when he first started the site; rather, he simply wanted a better learning experience than he was getting from his school. He now manages a 20-person team of programmers, designers, animators, and other professionals from all over the world, not including the experts who teach classes on the site. During the AMA, he said, "I am generating money. Just not profit." Though, I'm fairly certain things will soon change for this young man, who has big dreams and a deal with his parents. "If I make a million dollars before I turn 18," he says, "I don't have to go to college. I'm going to do it or die trying." He is currently continuing his education via homeschooling.

While this story, on the one hand is a success story about how people can turn a check from grandma into a six-figure profit, and use that money to start a business; on the other hand, this is a story about how public school is failing the students. This young man was not learning what he wanted to learn, nor was it being offered by the one-size-fits-all government school. He also wasn't able to find what he was looking for on sites like Khan Academy.

Finman told Business Insider[39], "I think of [Botangle] as an online institution. I'm working on making Botangle the best

---

39   Joey Cosco, *This 15-year-old kid made $100,000 from Bitcoin, then used it to launch his own startup*, (June 11, 2014),
http://www.businessinsider.com/15-year-old-kid-launches-education-startup-with-bitcoin-fortune-2014-6

website on the web for someone to completely leave the status quo education system and learn completely through the web!"

When it comes to the free market, education and starting a business, Finman has found that "you can create anything you want with no barrier to entry on the Internet."

But not everyone wants to, or has the capability to, learn via computer. And many parents still feel pressured to send their children to a government-funded school. However, most parents don't have a choice of which government-funded school their children attend. On the surface, the question about school choice seems obvious: should parents be allowed to choose which school their children attend? On the surface, it seems like the answer is obvious: YES!

A recent study by Troy University[40]seems to confirm this. Highlights from the School Choice works! Research shows that:
- Increasing the number and types of K-12 schools, and empowering parents to decide which is best for their children will lead to better academic outcomes...
- A one-size-fits-all approach fails to provide the necessary flexibility to encourage experimentation and to meet the diverse educational goals of parents and students.
- Evidence from school choice programs across the nation shows that even small doses of school choice boost school system performance.

The minutia comes about in the details of implementing school choice programs. The New Hampshire Supreme Court recently upheld a tax credit scholarship program that helps provide scholarships to children of low-income parents. The

---

40   Dr. John Merrifield and Jesse A. Ortiz Jr., *Reinventing the Alabama K-12 system to engage more children in productive learning,*
http://business.troy.edu/JohnsonCenter/reinventing-the-alabama-k-12-system-to-engage-more-children-in-productive-learning.aspx

A Rebel's Journey

Franklin Center reports,[41] "In New Hampshire, Business Tax Credits offer businesses a partial tax credit (85%) for donations made to organizations which provide scholarships to low-income families (defined as income less than 300% of the federal poverty line). It is then up to these families to determine what is best for them: tuition-charging public schools in nearby districts, homeschool, or tuition at a private school, including those which have religious affiliations and instruction."

In other states, the money comes directly from the state or local government in the form of vouchers. Along with the voucher comes strings. Meaning that once a private school, whether religious or not, receives the tax-payer money, the schools are then put further under the control of a government. Many people will look no deeper than these attached strings, and decide at that point whether or not to support school choice. Some will look only at the fact that tax-payer money is possibly being transferred to religious private schools, and decide to oppose school choice.

Few people look at the fact that government-run schooling is a wealth redistribution program. The National Center for Education Statistics[42] estimates the current per student expenditure to be $12,281 for the 2014–15 school year. The source of this funding varies from state-to-state, though most states will use property, income and/or sales taxes to fund[43] government-run schools. Government-run schools, as with all things government-run, require that (almost) everyone pay for a program that not (almost) everyone uses. The only sure-fire way to have real school choice, is to remove government from the

41   Amelia Hamilton, *New Hampshire Supreme Court rules for school choice*, (September 3, 2014),
http://watchdogwire.com/blog/2014/09/03/new-hampshire-supreme-court-rules-school-choice/
42   National Center for Education Statistics, *Back to school statistics*,
http://nces.ed.gov/fastfacts/display.asp?id=372
43   New America Foundation, *Federal Education Budget Project*, (April 21, 2014),
http://febp.newamerica.net/background-analysis/school-finance

equation. As long as people are being forced to pay for schools they don't want to use, there is no real choice.

AFTERWORD

There are many other issues that I could write about, including but not limited to: monetary policy and the Federal Reserve, secession, states rights, intellectual property, energy, and health care. If you had a friend drive from New York to Los Angeles, you wouldn't want to hear about every billboard they passed, every bug they hit, and every meal they ate along the way. You'd want to hear about the time they met someone famous at a corner diner in Indiana. You'd want to hear about the unexpected detour they took to see Pike's Peak, and the Four Corner's Monument. Similarly, this book is intended to serve as a guide to the highlights of my path to the ideas of liberty.

Speaking of detours, however, there are a few things that I wanted to include in the book that fit in neither the introduction, nor in any of the chapters.

Activism

Let me begin by saying that I've been a self-described news junkie since my teen years. Even before I was old enough to vote, I would make calls to my member of Congress to express a view. However, I would not say that doing so makes one an activist per se. In my early twenties, I began writing letters to the editor of local newspapers, and began emailing articles to friends – this was before blogging was a thing. I even ran for office several times as a means to raise awareness about various issues.

However, I did not consider myself to be an activist until 2007; and I still clearly remember the moment I became an activist. In March 2007, the Alabama Legislature voted itself a 62% pay raise, which the Governor vetoed. However, the leadership in the Alabama Legislature decided they would vote to override that veto. Obviously this garnered the attention of the media. Not only had the Legislature voted themselves a pay raise, the manner in which they did it was very sneaky. On the morning in which the bill was approved by the Senate, the Lt. Governor was reading a list of monotonous bills in a monotone voice. After the vote was taken, one Senator asked another if they just voted themselves a pay raise, and immediately called for a roll call vote. Even though several Republican Senators raised their hands requesting a recorded vote, Lt. Governor Jim Folsom Jr. said he neither saw nor heard anyone ask for a roll call vote. If that's not enough, the pay raise was not on the agendas of the House or Senate on the morning of the vote.[44]

Two weeks later, the vote to override the veto was on the agenda. Local media organized a protest in front of the Alabama Statehouse for the morning of March 20, 2007. I made the 90 mile drive from Birmingham to Montgomery to join others in a public display of opposition to this pay raise, and to personally deliver the message to my Senator and Representative that what they were doing was a blatant abuse of power.

After rally, that upwards of 200 people attended, I went into the Statehouse to speak with the people who were supposed to be

---

44   David White and Kim Chandlers, *Legislators vote selves more than 60% raise; Riley promises veto,* (March 8, 2007),
http://blog.al.com/spotnews/2007/03/legislators_vote_selves_more_t.html

representing me. My Representative was not in his office, so I wasn't able to deliver my message to him, though I caught my Senator as she was leaving her office. Walking down the hallway, I told her that the State Constitution had provisions on legislative pay, and if she wanted more than what was authorized by the constitution to pass an amendment. She replied, "if we amend the constitution, then the voters have to approve it. And you won't give me a pay raise!"

I responded, "not a 62% pay raise! If you're going to give yourself a pay raise, do it the right way!" By this time, about five other Senators appeared near the elevator and I was asked why I was harassing the Senator. Can you believe that? Speaking to your supposed representative was considered harassment by these other Senators? The Senators got on the elevator as I explained that I wasn't harassing anyone, rather telling my Senator to vote against overriding the veto. By that afternoon, both houses of the Alabama Legislature has voted to override the veto.[45]

Since that fateful Tuesday, I have volunteered to serve as precinct coordinator for the Ron Paul 2008 Presidential campaign; I was the county coordinator for a brief period for the We The People Foundation; I founded and co-chaired the Alabama affiliate of the Boston Tea Party; served on the National Committee of the Boston Tea Party as an At-Large member from 2008-2010, and as Chair from 2010-2012; and in 2012 helped co-found the New Hampshire Liberty Party. I've organized tax-day protests, anti-war rallies, and rallies in support of whistleblowers.

After moving to New Hampshire in 2012, as part of the Free State Project,[46] I began attending legislative committee hearings,

---

45   David White, *Lawmakers override Riley's veto of pay raise*, (March 20, 2007), http://blog.al.com/spotnews/2007/03/house_overrides_rileys_veto_of.html

46   The Free State Project is an effort to recruit 20,000 liberty-loving people to move to New Hampshire. We are looking for neighborly, productive, tolerant folks from any and all walks of life, of all ages, creeds, and colors, who agree to the political

and testifying on legislation. This is probably one of the easiest things to do, and in many ways more rewarding than holding a one-man tax protest. Last year I had the idea to adopt a legislative committee, and serve as a shadow legislator.[47] During the first year of the legislative term, I attended almost every hearing held by the Election Law Committee of the New Hampshire Legislature, testified on the vast majority of the bills they heard, and had a better attendance record than half of the members of the committee. Because of this "citizen lobbying" I've had State Reps approach me in the hallway of the Legislative Office Building to ask me questions about bills in other committees. I've also seen State Reps in random places, and begun conversations about possible legislation. These conversations would not have been possible had I not gone to the Statehouse on a regular basis.

Aside from testifying to legislators, there are other ways to challenge laws and statutes. One such way is civil disobedience. I do not recommend anyone supporting a family commit acts of civil disobedience, because chances are you will either pay a fine which could have otherwise been used to feed, clothe and house your family, or you will go to jail. I also don't recommend committing civil disobedience if you are not prepared and willing to get arrested.

It's not often that an act of civil disobedience leads to a situation where a court decides to overturn the law or a legislative body decides to repeal the law, though it has happened. Forced

---

philosophy expressed in our Statement of Intent: "I hereby state my solemn intent to move to the State of New Hampshire. Once there, I will exert the fullest practical effort toward the creation of a society in which the maximum role of government is the protection of individuals' rights to life, liberty, and property." Anyone who promotes violence, racial hatred, or bigotry is not welcome.
http://FreeStateProject.org

47   I've tried to find others willing and able to adopt a committee. This would involve reading and reviewing every bill in the committee; attending as many hearing as possible, and testifying on most of the bills.

A Rebel's Journey

segregation is just one example of laws that were repealed because of civil disobedience.

While the term was popularized by Henry David Thoreau, the concept is much older, dating back to at least Socrates, who vowed in T*he Apology* that he will disobey the lawful jury if it orders him to stop philosophizing. Thoreau's conception of civil disobedience has two principles. The first is that the authority of the government depends on the consent of the governed. The second is that justice is superior to the laws enacted by the government, and the individual has the right to judge whether a given law reflects or flouts justice. In the latter case the individual has the duty to disobey the law and accept the consequences of the disobedience nonviolently.

Another hero of civil disobedience, Ghandi, called his practice "satyagraha," a Gujarati word meaning "firmness in adhering to truth." Satyagraha, free of the defects of passive resistance, introduced six elements into the theory and practice of civil disobedience.[48] For Gandhi, it was not enough to seek to improve the state; it was equally necessary to seek to improve civil society.

---

48   First, its moral basis was grounded in truth, a basis much deeper than that provided by the theory of consent. To be binding, laws had to be truthful. All untruthful laws had to be resisted, though civilly—that is, by truthful means.

Second, civil disobedience presupposed the obligation to obey the state: only those had the right to practice civil disobedience who knew "how to offer voluntary and deliberate obedience" to the laws of the state.

Third, commitment to nonviolence was an essential component of civil disobedience. The commitment in question could be either moral or tactical, depending on the moral aptitude of the practitioner.

Fourth, the practice of civil disobedience required a minimum degree of moral fitness, to be acquired by the exercise of such virtues as truthfulness, nonviolence, temperance, courage, fearlessness, and freedom from greed.

Fifth, a practitioner of civil disobedience had to accept the punishment consequent to the disobedience voluntarily, and without complaint.

Finally, engagement in civil disobedience had to be complemented by engagement in organized social work.

Darryl W. Perry

So, the next time you have a chance to, please practice Satyagraha, remember that it is your right, nay, your duty to stand up for your rights, your freedom and your liberty. I say this as someone who has refused to comply with arbitrary laws. I have gone to court several times for non-violent offenses that had no victim. In 2010, I took a ticket for a seatbelt violation to a jury trial. I attempted to persuade the jury to nullify the law because of Supreme Court precedent, but was threatened with contempt of court no less than five times. I was able to get the officer to tell the jury that I had told him I practice civil disobedience, and he even admitted that he had no physical evidence that I wasn't wearing my seatbelt. Nonetheless, I was still found guilty by the jury in about five minutes.

I've taken tickets for expired registration to court, I lost both times, though I was allowed to perform community service in lieu of the fine once. The second time, in a different court, I was not allowed to perform community service and instead was sentenced to 72 hours in jail. Upon my release, I immediately said, "I was not corrected!"

I will continue to stand up for my rights, and disobey unjust laws, and will encourage others to do the same!

As an aside: there are some people who believe that activists should be paid for their activism, and that activism will only happen if people are financially incentivized. While I'm not opposed to people donating to activities and causes they like, there should not be an expectation of financial reward for activism. I did not become an activist because I was being paid. I became an activist because I wanted to make a difference, and I could afford to do activism. I would not be doing everything I am today, if I were driven solely by financial motives.

A Rebel's Journey

Publishing

As stated earlier, I've considered myself a news junkie for the majority of my life, and I have an Associates degree in Mass Communications. While in college, I got a a job working as a board operator for a pair of radio stations, one was sports talk, the other was news talk. My job was to play the commercials during the various sports broadcasts, this was before computers were able to automate that task. At the time, I was dreaming of being a sports broadcaster, though as the sports cliché goes: life threw me a curve ball.

After a falling out with the Program Director – he wasn't happy that I went over his head after he forgot to turn in my time sheet a couple of times – I got a job as a traffic reporter. As fate would have it, one of my assignments was the pair of stations I had just left. For the next 6 months, I would report the traffic on about half a dozen stations as Miles Marker – it was common at the time for traffic reporters to use a traffic related pseudonym.

Then in the Summer of 1999, I decided to chase love, and moved to Pennsylvania. For the next several years, I tried off and on to get back into the radio business, but was told numerous times that I was either over-qualified or under-qualified for the position, and I began to think of broadcasting as just a phase in my life.

In 2008 when I was working for a subsidiary of Delta Airlines I took trip to Washington DC. After landing, my plans changed, so I decided to visit the Newseum. Visiting the Newseum reignited something in me, though it would be nearly a year later before the inspiration would be put into action. The primary inspiration was a single quote on one of the walls: "Freedom of the press is guaranteed only to those who own one." ~ A. J. Liebling. A few months earlier, I began writing monthly commentary for the website NolanChart.com; around the same time, I was writing a series of articles based on interviews with minor party Presidential candidates. Coincidentally, I interviewed Constitution Party Presidential nominee Chuck Baldwin on my phone, in a stairwell of the Newseum. But, that quote stuck with me. "What," I thought to myself, "would happen if the website I'm writing for shuts down? What if the newspapers stop printing letters to the editor? What if the local talk radio shows stop taking callers?"

It was my quest to find an answer that led me to create my own media outlets, with the purpose of ensuring a free press for the freedom movement. I wanted to ensure not just my own freedom of the press, but that of everyone else who valued liberty. I wanted to not only provide an online platform, but a physical platform as well, through books and other print media[49]. In early 2009, I was asked to provide weekly commentary for the unofficial newspaper of West Virginia University. So, by the time FPP was launched, I had been creating regular content for several months. And a couple of months before launching FPP, I edited and published *Songs of Freedom: Tales from the Revolution* as a tribute to the Ron Paul 2008 campaign. This book would later be named one of four finalist in the Current Events: Political/Social category of the "Best Books 2010" Awards and was selected Book of the Month for August 2009 by Freedom Book Club. *The Anarcho Teachings of Yeshua,* which was published in 2010, won awards from Freedom Book Club and LAVA[50].

In 2011, I found out about podcasting, and began creating audio versions of my weekly commentary into short podcasts. Several months later, I was listening to Free Talk Live, and heard Ian Freeman mention that he'd like to replace the Fox News five-minute radio newscast that aired at the top of the hour on the Liberty Radio Network (LRN.fm). I contacted him about airing

---

49   The newsletter that became the newspaper was first published in May 2010.

50   The Libertarian, Agorist, Voluntarist and Anarchs Authors and Publishers Association

the *FPP Freedom Minute*, and was given some tips on how to improve the quality of the audio so it would sound good on the air. After moving to New Hampshire in April 2012 I was allowed to use the LRN.fm studio for recording, which meant for the first time since 1999, I had the ability to use professional recording equipment. I was also invited to be a co-host on *Free Talk Live*, and in October 2013 began working for *Free Talk Live* doing affiliate relations. By December 2012 I began hosting by own weekly 2-hour talk show on LRN.fm, *Peace, Love, Liberty Radio*, in addition to the *FPP Freedom Minute*; and in February 2014 began producing a daily five-minute newscast: *FPPRadioNews*.

Over the Summer of 2012, what had been a newsletter that was mailed to subscribers became a monthly newspaper that was distributed via newspaper racks across New Hampshire. I joined the cast of *Free Keene TV*, which later became *Shire TV*, which later morphed into *Black Sheep Rising*.

My adult life, which began with me pursuing a degree in broadcasting, has through a series of detours, led me to owning my own media duchy.[51]

Final thoughts

You have traveled with this rebel on his path to liberty. However my journey is not over. There are still many miles ahead of me, and just as my journey did not begin on the day I was born, my journey will not end on the day that I die, whenever that may be in the future. As long as there is air to breathe, there will be someone with the rebel spirit to continue my journey. Because my journey is a rebel's journey, and a rebel's journey never ends!

---

51 FPP is by no means large enough to consider a media empire. Duchy is five steps below Empire in the rank of royal and noble titles.

ABOUT THE AUTHOR

Darryl has spent most of his adult life as an advocate & activist for peace and liberty.

Darryl is an award winning author, publisher & radio/TV host, and is a regular contributor to several weekly and monthly newspapers. He hosts several podcasts, and is a regular co-host on *Free Talk Live*.

Darryl is a co-founder of the NH Liberty Party, and was on the National Committee of the Boston Tea Party from 2008-2012. He was the longest serving member of the National Committee, and was twice elected Chair. The BTP dissolved in July 2012 after he resigned as Chair.

Darryl is the Owner/Managing Editor of Free Press Publications, a business he started in June, 2009 with the purpose of ensuring a FREE PRESS for the FREEDOM MOVEMENT. Since then FPP has republished several libertarian classics as well as new books, both fiction and non-fiction, many of which have won awards and other recognition.

Darryl is running for President in 2016 to spread the message of peace, freedom, love & liberty!